FEEL THE FORCE

Win that SPRINT!

Forces in Sport

Angela Royston

raintree

Raintree is an imprint of Capstone Global Library Limited, a company incorporated in England and Wales having its registered office at 7 Pilgrim Street, London, EC4V 6LB – Registered company number: 6695582

www.raintree.co.uk
myorders@raintree.co.uk

Text © Capstone Global Library Limited 2016
The moral rights of the proprietor have been asserted.

Edited by Helen Cox Cannons and Holly Beaumont
Designed by Philippa Jenkins
Original illustrations © Capstone Global Library Ltd
Illustrated by HL Studios, Witney, Oxon; page 7 Medi-mation; page 16 Barry Atkinson
Picture research by Tracy Cummins
Production by Helen McCreath
Originated by Capstone Global Library Ltd
Printed and Bound in China by Leo Paper Group

ISBN 978 1 406 29646 4 (hardback)
19 18 17 16 15
10 9 8 7 6 5 4 3 2 1

ISBN 978 1 406 29651 8 (paperback)
20 19 18 17 16
10 9 8 7 6 5 4 3 2 1

British Library Cataloguing in Publication Data
A full catalogue record for this book is available from the British Library.

Acknowledgements
We would like to thank the following for permission to reproduce photographs: Adidas-Salomon AG: 36; Capstone Press: Barry Atkinson, 16, HL Studios, 6 Top, Karon Dubke, 10, 11, 18, 19, 22, 23, Medi-mation, 7; Corbis: 237/Robert Daly/Ocean, 34; Dreamstime: Amy S. Myers, 38, James Phelps Jr, 35, Photographerlondon, 24, 43 Middle, Sarah Dusautoir, 25; Getty Images: Asad Zaidi/Bloomberg, 37; iStockphotos: technotr, 14, 42 Bottom; Shutterstock: Andrey Myagkov, Design Element, bikeriderlondon, 20, 31, Diego Barbieri, 15, ev radin, 41, FCG, 12, 42 Top, Gustavo Miguel Fernandes, 17, Herbert Kratky, 28, Iurii Osadchi, 27, Jacek Chabraszewski, 13, Michael Mitchell, 6 Bottom, 43 Top, muzsy, 29, Natursports, 39, oliveromg, 26, Paolo Bona, 33, Pete Saloutos, Front Cover, Peter Bernik, 8, 9, 42 Middle; Thinkstock: Daniel Hurst, 4, Dilip Vishwanat, 32, 43 Bottom, Yie Sandison, 5.

We would like to thank Patrick O'Mahony for his invaluable help in the preparation of this book.

Every effort has been made to contact copyright holders of material reproduced in this book. Any omissions will be rectified in subsequent printings if notice is given to the publisher.

All the internet addresses (URLs) given in this book were valid at the time of going to press. However, due to the dynamic nature of the internet, some addresses may have changed, or sites may have changed or ceased to exist since publication. While the author and publisher regret any inconvenience this may cause readers, no responsibility for any such changes can be accepted by either the author or the publisher.

Contents

Some words are shown in bold, **like this**. You can find
out what they mean by looking in the glossary.

What makes a winner?

Sport is a good way to exercise and become healthier, but competing to win is what makes sport so exciting. Athletes and teams pit their strength and skill against each other. The winners are those who can best use their bodies to produce **forces** and control them.

Making it happen

A force is needed to get something moving and to keep it moving, but forces can do much more than that. They can make an object change direction. They can make it change speed or stop moving. Forces can even make an object change shape. Every movement or change in movement needs a force to make it happen.

Who wins the race? Generally, the fastest runner is the person who can produce the strongest force to push them across the finish line first.

FORCES IN ACTION

A force is either a push or a pull. When you hit or throw a ball, you push it in the direction you want it to go. In swimming, you pull yourself through the water. As you compete in a race or game, you are generating and using many different forces to get the result you want.

A player throws the ball accurately to score a goal. To do this he has to control the force that makes the ball move.

Forces in sport

In most sports, the competitors produce the forces needed for every movement in the race or game. Athletes race to see who can run, jump or swim the fastest. Many ball games, such as football, basketball and rugby, involve two teams playing against each other. In tennis, cricket and other games, the players hit the ball with a racket or a bat. This book looks at how athletes use different forces to make sport fast and skilful.

How does your body produce forces?

To move your body you have to move your bones. Bones, however, cannot move by themselves, and so they are attached to **muscles** that **contract**, or become shorter, to produce the force to pull the bones.

The main muscles you use to throw are in your shoulder and arm, although you also use muscles in your stomach, back and legs.

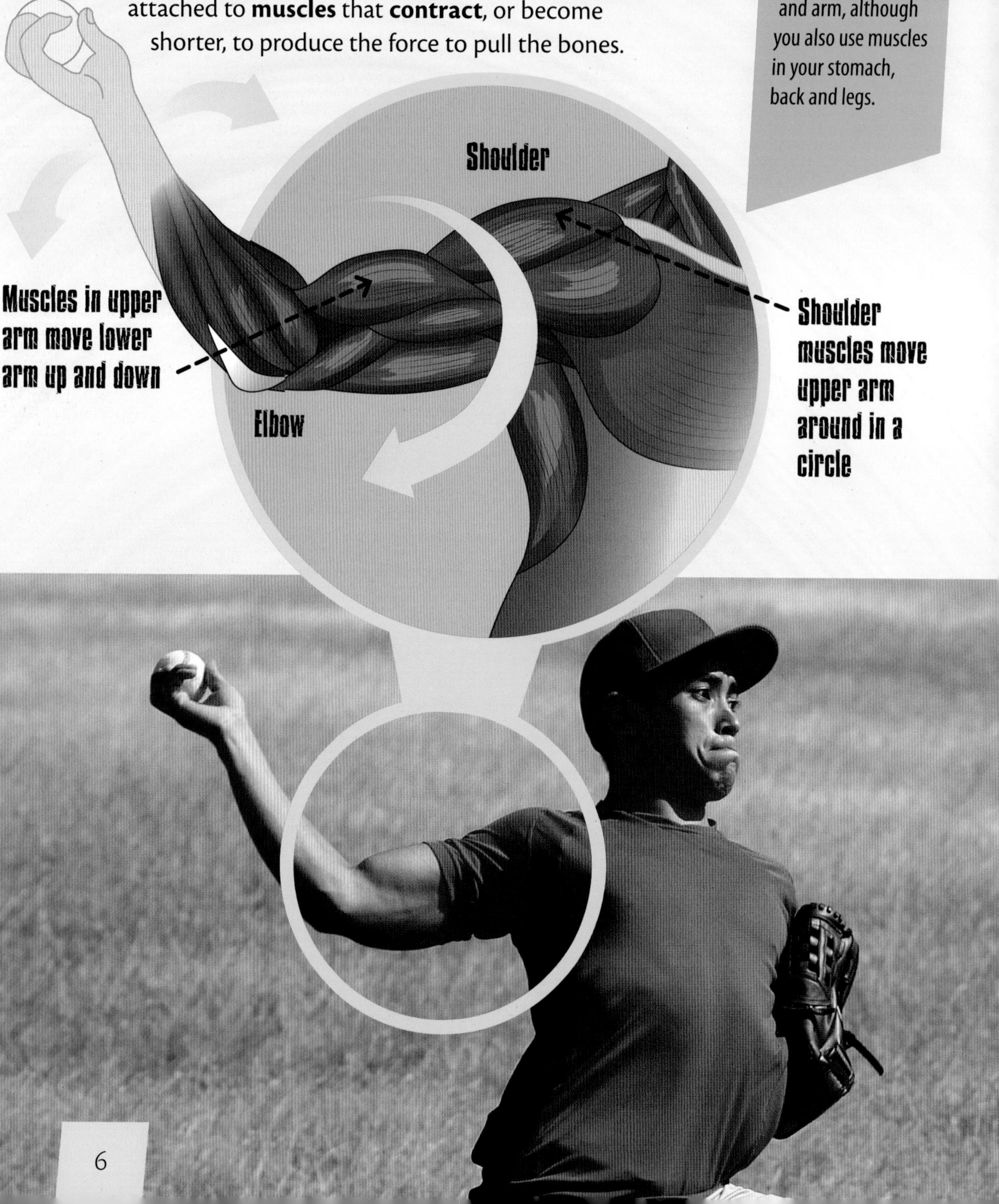

Shoulder
Muscles in upper arm move lower arm up and down
Elbow
Shoulder muscles move upper arm around in a circle

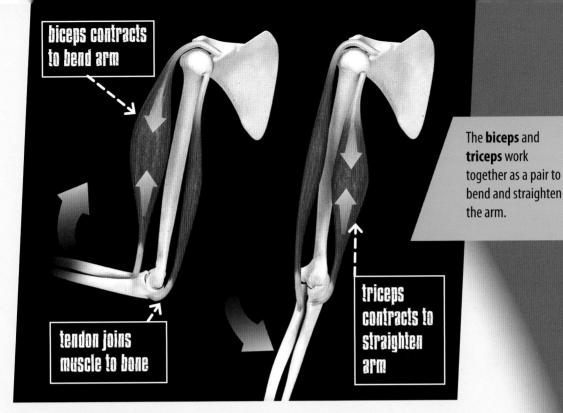

biceps contracts to bend arm

tendon joins muscle to bone

triceps contracts to straighten arm

The **biceps** and **triceps** work together as a pair to bend and straighten the arm.

Bones and joints

Your legs and arms are each made up of three long bones, one in the upper leg or arm and two in the lower leg or arm. A **joint** is the place where bones meet and it allows particular parts of the body to move. For example, the elbow is a joint that allows your lower arm to move, while your shoulder joint allows your upper arm to move.

Muscles

Muscles cannot push a bone, they can only pull it. They move a bone by pulling it across a joint. For example, two muscles in your upper arm move the bones in your lower arm to bend and straighten your elbow. To throw a ball, muscles in the back and shoulders pull your arm around in a big circle, before muscles in the upper arm straighten the arm as you throw.

Practice

Exercise makes the muscles and bones stronger and helps the joints to move more easily. Top athletes spend many hours a day exercising and practising, but exercise makes everyone fitter and healthier.

How do sprinters run so fast?

A sprint is a fast race over a short distance. Sprinters launch themselves from the starting blocks, accelerate to top speed and pound down the track. The fastest sprinters cover 100 metres (328 feet) in less than 10 seconds. The winner is the person who can best use their muscles and coordinate the movement of their legs and arms to propel themselves forward.

The starting blocks

Before the race begins, sprinters take their place at the start. They crouch down with each foot against a sloping starting block, and bend forward with their fingertips on the start line. As the starting pistol fires, the sprinters push against the blocks and use their thighs, **hips** and **glutes** (from the Latin name *gluteus maximi*, for the muscles that form the buttocks) to force themselves upwards and forwards.

A sprinter waits on the starting blocks for the starter's pistol to fire. Their muscles are tense, ready to propel them towards the finish line.

The sprint

At every stride, the runner pushes backwards against the ground with one foot while the hip, glutes and thigh muscles lift and drive the other leg forwards. As the lifted leg stretches forwards and touches down, the calf muscles bend the foot, ready to push off with the next stride. One leg after the other repeats the sequence, while the opposite arms swing to keep the body balanced.

A sprinter uses the muscles in her thighs, calves, buttocks, hips, shoulders and upper arms to reach top speed from the start.

GETTING A GRIP

Muscle power is not the only force that runners rely on. They could not use their feet to grip and push off the ground without a force called **friction**. Friction slows down or prevents one surface moving against another. Without friction, the runners' feet would slip as they pushed backwards. Friction is greater or lesser depending on how rough or smooth the surfaces are.

ACTIVITY: Measuring friction

Use a **force meter** to measure the force of friction. Compare the amount of friction produced by rough- and smooth-soled shoes, and discover if dry or wet surfaces produce more. Remember, friction increases with weight, so to make this a fair test you'll need to make the shoes weigh the same.

You will need:

- a training shoe with a rough sole
- two shoes with different, smoother soles, such as a ballet shoe
- a force meter
- marbles
- a smooth floor or surface

1 Use the force meter to weigh each shoe and make a note of the weights.

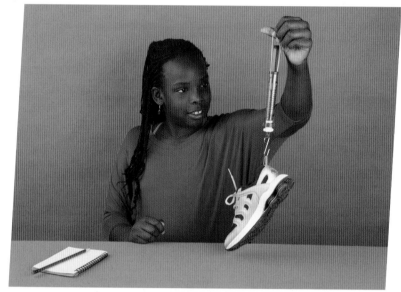

2 Put marbles inside the lighter shoes until all the shoes weigh the same.

3 Place one of the shoes on the smooth surface and hook the force meter to the top of the heel. Measure and record the force needed to move the shoe. Repeat with the other two shoes. Which shoe needs most force?

4 Wet the surface and measure the forces again. Are the forces larger or smaller than before? Record your results.

Conclusion

The training shoe has a rubbery sole with grooves running through it. It should have needed the largest force to make it move. The smoothest sole should have needed the least force. Water reduces friction, so less force should have been needed on the wet surface. The grooves help the shoe to grip in the wet, however, so the training shoe may still have taken a large force to make it move.

What makes a good long-distance runner?

While top sprinters are big and muscular, long-distance runners are usually slim and lightweight. They have strong running muscles and lots of **stamina** – the ability to keep going for a long time.

Fuelling the muscles

Muscles burn fuel to release **energy**. This energy can be used to create a force. The fuel is sugar, which comes from the food you eat and drink. The **oxygen** needed to burn the fuel comes from the air you breathe into your **lungs**. To keep working, the muscles need a constant supply of fuel and oxygen.

A marathon race is 42.2 kilometres (26.2 miles) long. Runners drink energy drinks as they run to keep their muscles topped up with energy food.

Heart and lungs

Long-distance runners develop strong hearts and good lungs. The heart is made up of muscles that contract and relax to pump blood all around the body. On the way, the blood collects sugar and **nutrients** from the **digestive system** and oxygen from the lungs. It then delivers these to the muscles and other parts of the body.

Improving delivery

Athletes increase their stamina by exercising their heart and lungs during **aerobic** exercise. Long-distance runners breathe in more air with every breath and their heart pushes more blood around the body with every beat. They can do this because the muscles that control breathing and form the heart are large and very strong.

Running is brilliant exercise. It strengthens the muscles and makes the heart and lungs work better. The more you practise running, the faster and further you will be able to go.

How can I jump further and higher?

Jumping uses muscle power to push the body into the air. Long jumpers push themselves up and forwards. High jumpers try to push themselves high enough to clear a bar. To jump they have to overcome the force of **gravity**, the force that pulls everything towards the ground.

GRAVITY

Gravity is a force of attraction between two objects. The larger an object is, the greater the force. Earth is so large that its gravity overpowers other forces and pulls everything towards the ground. A jumper has to overcome the force of gravity to rise into the air. After their momentum drops to zero, gravity pulls them down again.

A long jumper brings both arms and legs forward to help her travel further before gravity succeeds in bringing her down to the ground.

The run-up

Both long jumpers and high jumpers run up to the jump. Running helps them to go on moving through the air. This force is called **momentum** and is a combination of an object's **mass** and speed. Long jumpers and high jumpers run forwards before taking off so that their momentum will carry them further or higher.

The jump

When they reach the point of take-off, they bend the take-off leg and push down with the foot. As they straighten the leg, they push off into the air. A long jumper stretches their feet forwards and tries to pull the rest of the body forwards before they land. A high jumper uses their momentum to travel upwards. They twist their body in the air so that their head goes over the bar first, followed by their back and legs. It is vital that a high jumper has a safe place to land.

This style of high jump is called the Fosbury Flop, after the high jumper Dick Fosbury who used it to win a gold medal in the 1968 Olympic Games.

Pole-vaulting

The highest jumpers are pole-vaulters. Top high jumpers can clear over 2.4 metres (nearly 8 feet), but top pole-vaulters reach over 6 metres (20 feet). They could not do it without a pole, which stores their energy and **levers** them over the bar.

LEVERS

A lever uses a force, called the **effort**, to lift a **load**. The lever turns around a point called the **pivot** and this is what makes the force more effective. A first-class lever has the pivot between the effort and the load. A pole vault pole acts as a second-class lever. The effort comes from the vaulter pushing upwards with their foot and upper hand.

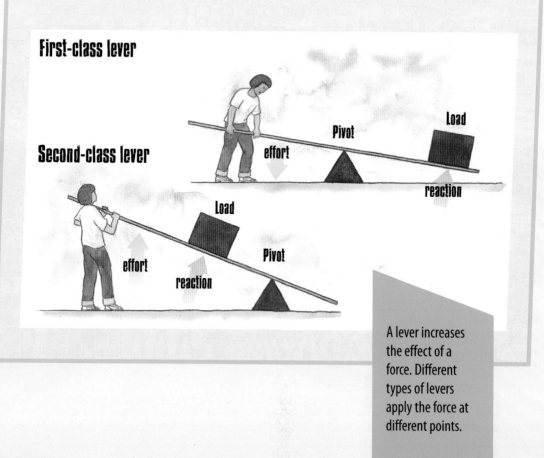

First-class lever

Second-class lever

Load

Pivot

effort

reaction

Load

effort

reaction

Pivot

A lever increases the effect of a force. Different types of levers apply the force at different points.

A pole vaulter uses the momentum gained in the run-up to lift her into the air. The pole then helps to lever her over the bar.

Higher and higher

First, the vaulter runs up to the jump, carrying the pole so that it points forwards. As they slide the front of the pole into a special box, the pole bends. The vaulter then pushes off the ground with their lower foot while their top hand pushes the top of the pole up. They swing their hips and legs above their head and half turn to swing over the bar.

The role of the pole

The pole acts as a lever, which magnifies a force to give a bigger effect. The pole turns around the end in the box, moving the top of the pole a long way. But the pole does more than that. The pole stores the energy used to bend it. As the pole straightens, the energy returns to the vaulter, giving them an extra push to lift themselves higher.

Load

Lever

Pivot
where the pole touches the ground

ACTIVITY: How a vaulter's pole works

Use rulers to show how a pole vaulter's pole works. Vaulters use the pole to give themselves as much height as possible, but this experiment uses bendy rulers to give distance. Measure how far different rulers project a pen top to find out which one works best.

!

SAFETY! When you release the ruler, take care not to hit yourself, or anyone else with the pen top.

1 Mark a starting point on a table top or on the floor. Put the shortest ruler upright on the mark and place the pen top at the top of the ruler so that the pointed end is facing forwards. Bend the ruler back.

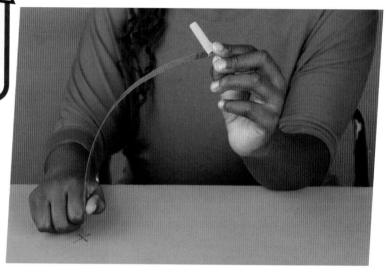

2 Release the top of the ruler so that the pen top is projected through the air. Measure how far the pen top travelled. Have three goes and record the result each time.

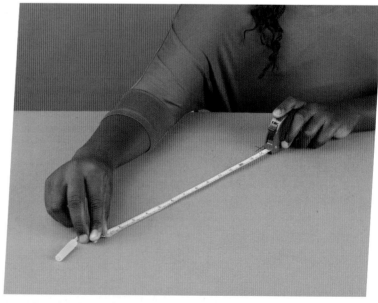

3 Repeat with the middle-sized ruler. Does the pen top travel further or less far than before?

4 Repeat with the longest ruler. Does it catapult the pen top further or less far? Which ruler is best of all? Is it longer or shorter, bendier or more rigid than the other rulers?

Conclusion

Long levers require less force than shorter levers, so the longest ruler may fire the pen top further. The bendiest ruler will store more energy than more rigid rulers. However, the bendiest ruler may fire the pen top at too steep an angle, so that it goes up rather than along. The best ruler will be the one that fires the pen top at an angle about half-way between the floor and the upright. Pole-vaulters have to get their angles right too!

Why is swimming slower than running?

Straight arm enters water

Arm pushes back along body

Body is streamlined and head is in line with body

Legs kick water away

In backstroke, the arms and hands push the water towards your feet, pushing you forwards.

EQUAL RESISTANCE

Isaac Newton (1643–1727) was a brilliant scientist who worked out the laws of forces and motion and published them in 1687. His third law states that "for every action there is an equal and opposite **reaction**". This means that the greater the force you can produce to push the water backwards, the greater the force with which the water will push you forwards.

In swimming, you use your arms as well as your legs to move forwards, so why can you run faster than you can swim? The answer is that **water resistance** holds you back. As you move through the water, it pushes back against you, slowing you down. Air also pushes back when you run, but **air resistance** is weaker than water resistance.

Water resistance

Water resistance acts against any movement through water and slows you down. **Streamlining** helps to reduce water resistance. A fish has a streamlined shape because its body curves smoothly from its head to its tail and allows the water to flow easily around it.

Increasing speed

Streamlining helps you swim faster. In breaststroke, you move both hands forward together, so they cut through the water like the pointed bow of a boat. In all swimming strokes, you should keep your head in the water, in line with the rest of your body so that the water can flow smoothly over and around you. The exceptions are breaststroke and butterfly, when your head comes out of the water as your arms go back, allowing you to breathe.

ACTIVITY: Water resistance

Explore the effects of water resistance and get hands-on with modelling clay to find the most streamlined shape for moving through the water fastest.

You will need:
- a large plastic container or large, empty drinks bottle with the top cut off
- a chunk of modelling clay
- a stopwatch
- some water

1 Use the modelling clay to make a round ball about 2.5 centimetres (1 inch) across. Hold the ball above the lip of the container and time how long it takes to fall from the top to the bottom of the empty container.

2 Fill the container with water and time how long the ball takes to drop the same distance.

3 Now use the same chunk of clay to make the shape of a shark, whale or torpedo, which is pointed at one end. Time how long it takes to drop it through the water.

4 Change the shape of the modelling clay to make a flat "S" shape. How long does it take to drop down through the water? Which shape sank fastest? Which one sank slowest? Test other shapes to see if you can find one that is even faster.

Conclusion

The round ball should take longer to drop through water than through air, because water is more resistant than air. The pointed end of the cylinder shape makes it streamlined, like a shark or a torpedo, so it should fall fastest. The bent, flat "S" shape is like a person swimming with their head out of the water and their legs drooping. It should take longer to fall. Did you find a faster shape? Could you copy that shape when you swim?

What muscles and joints do I use to swim?

Swimming is one of the healthiest sports because it uses all the main groups of muscles. The muscles in the shoulders, back and upper arms move the arms, and those in the hips, glutes and legs move the legs. In front crawl and backstroke, the arms move one at a time. In breaststroke, both arms and then both legs move together.

Moving your arms

In front crawl, you bend one arm, turn it forwards and straighten the elbow to stretch the arm as it enters the water. As you pull the arm through the water, the lower arm flexes your wrist so that the palm of your hand is flat against the water. As one arm moves through the water, the other arm repeats the movement.

This swimmer is making herself as streamlined as possible. Her outstretched arm cuts through the water and one leg pushes water down, while the rest of her body stays in a straight line.

Moving your legs

The movement of the legs also drives the swimmer forwards. In front crawl, you bend and straighten first one knee and then the other. As the leg straightens, you pull the thigh down to increase the force pushing the water away.

Pushing off or diving in

Top swimmers achieve extra speed by diving forwards into the water at the start of a race and so gain extra momentum. In a swimming pool, you can also get extra momentum by pushing off from the edge of the pool.

At the start of a race, swimmers dive in, their streamlined shapes slicing through the water.

Why do sledges move so fast?

Sledging is thrilling, both to do and to watch as a sport. The fastest sledges are bobsleighs. These speed down a narrow, icy slope, going fastest where the slope is steepest. Two natural forces help sledges to go fast: the force of gravity increases and maintains their speed, while the slippery ice decreases friction, keeping the sledge moving.

Sledging on a snowy hill is fun. Some people have proper toboggans but others use any smooth surface, such as a kitchen tray or plastic bag!

A bobsleigh team pushes off at the top of the slope then jump quickly into their sleigh before it rockets down the track.

Pushing off

Human power provides the force to get a sledge moving. Ordinary sledgers sit on the sledge and push off with their feet, or are given a push by a friend. With a bobsleigh, the sleigh is pushed by the riders who run forward with it before jumping on board.

Fast track

A modern bobsleigh track is extremely smooth and includes a straight section as well as 15 or more bends. The track is made of concrete covered with ice, and the sleigh can travel at over 130 kilometres (80 miles) per hour. Riders bend down to make a more streamlined shape. They wear crash helmets and other protective clothes, but the sport is still dangerous.

REDUCING FRICTION

Friction is less between smooth surfaces than between rough surfaces. Sledges move on smooth runners over slippery ice, which reduces friction between them. In other situations, such as car engines, oil is used as a **lubricant**. This means that a film of oil is spread between two surfaces to make them smoother and so reduce friction.

How does ice skating work?

Ice skaters can move fast, spin on the spot and glide on one skate. Ice hockey is an extremely fast game, played between two teams with sticks and a rubber puck. Ice hockey and skating competitions usually take place on ice rinks, where the ice is smooth and slippery. The blades of ice skates are also smooth, reducing friction further.

Ice skating requires power and balance, strong leg muscles and stretchy joints.

FAST ICE

Ice is more slippery than any other smooth surface because it is covered with an extremely thin layer of water, and water is a lubricant. Even very cold ice has this water-like layer. The amount of water increases as the blade slides over the ice, partly because of friction and because the weight of the skater melts the ice beneath the blades. Skaters talk about fast ice, which is hard ice, and soft ice, which is slushier. Soft ice is slower for skating on than hard ice.

Ice hockey players move fast and use their sticks to hit the puck to pass and to score goals. As the game goes on, the ice becomes softer and slushier.

Moving on skates

To skate, you push the blades of the skates against the ice to move yourself in the opposite direction. As one skate pushes, the other glides. The muscles in the thigh bend the knee and straighten it to push off. The glutes and hip muscles give more power, and the muscles around the stomach keep the skater stable.

Ice hockey

Top ice hockey players need to have quick reactions as well as strong muscles. One moment they are speeding in one direction, the next they have stopped and are dodging opposing players before passing the puck. A player leans forward and digs his skates into the ice to accelerate.

How can I throw further?

Games such as cricket, rounders and netball involve throwing a ball, and athletes compete to throw a javelin, discus and shot the furthest. The greater the force behind the throw the further the object will go. The forces that work against the throw are air resistance and gravity.

The throw

To throw a ball forwards, you push it with force from your muscles (see page 6). Taking your arm back first means that as you swing your arm forwards you are applying the force for a longer time. Flexing your wrist as you release puts extra force behind the ball. Running up to make the throw passes more momentum to the ball.

The forces against

Air resistance is the force of the air pushing against a moving ball or object. Air resistance slows the ball while gravity pulls it towards the ground. To **counteract** gravity, you need to throw the ball upwards as well as forwards. If you throw it too steeply, the ball will go up instead of forwards. If you throw it straight ahead, gravity will soon bring it down to the ground. You need to throw the ball halfway between the vertical and the horizontal – at an angle of about 45 degrees.

Path of the ball

As the ball travels forwards, its path makes an arc through the air. It rises most steeply at first and then flattens out. As it falls, it continues to move forwards, until it hits the ground.

To throw a ball well, the thrower has to coordinate the movement of their entire body with the movement of their throwing arm.

Ball is released at the top of the forward swing

As throwing arm swings forwards, the other arm swings back to balance movement

Standing with feet far apart aids stability as weight moves from back to front foot

Catch that ball!

To catch a ball you have to stop it moving, and then hold on to it without dropping it or letting it bounce out of your hands. To stop a force you have to meet it with an equal force in the opposite direction. The good news is that the force of friction is on your side when you catch a ball, and you can use it to make catching easier.

Catching gloves

In football, the goalkeeper wears thick gloves on both hands, but in baseball, the catcher has one cupped glove. The gloves are rough, which increases the friction between the surface of the ball and the gloves. Friction makes it easier to grip the ball and hold on to it.

The catcher gets himself into the right position, with the open end of the glove tilted to recover and grip the ball.

The catch

To make a successful catch you first have to get yourself in the right place. This involves judging the arc of the ball and positioning yourself so that you can catch the ball before it hits the ground. If you are catching with two hands, hold your hands pressed together just below the wrists so that the ball does not slip between them. As you catch the ball, pull it towards you. This takes some of the energy out of the ball as it slows down and stops.

Hard to catch

Wet balls are more slippery than dry ones, which means it is harder for goalkeepers to catch a ball when it is raining or the pitch is wet. Rugby balls are oval, not round. It is extra hard to catch them after they have bounced because then it is difficult to predict which way they will go!

What makes a ball bounce?

Many games or points in games are won or lost on the bounce of the ball. Most objects, such as books, tomatoes and shoes, hardly bounce at all, but round balls can bounce back almost to the point they started from. What is it that makes a ball so different?

Storing energy

When a ball hits a surface such as the ground, the surface pushes back with an equal but opposite force to send the ball in the opposite direction. A ball, however, is slightly squashy. The part that touches the surface is squashed, or **compressed**, as the ball comes to a rapid halt. The energy used to compress the ball is stored. As the ball returns to its original shape, the energy becomes a force that bounces the ball in the opposite direction.

Spinning and slicing

If you hit or kick an approaching ball flat in the middle, it will return and bounce along the same path. However, if you hit or kick the ball forward but off-centre, the ball will spin, making it curve and bounce to the left or right after it hits the ground. Tennis players often hit up and over the ball. This is called topspin and it brings the ball down sooner and makes it bounce higher.

The bottom of a bouncy ball is flattened as the ball hits the ground. This will give it extra energy on the rebound.

In tennis, a player hits a slice or underspin by hitting under the ball. This stroke slows the ball down and makes it change direction after it bounces.

CHANGING DIRECTION

If a ball is travelling fast, holding a bat or racket in its way stops the ball, and makes it **rebound** in the direction the bat or racket is pointing. Moving or swinging the racket or bat as it connects with the ball makes the ball rebound with added speed.

How is a football made?

It takes a lot of careful design and engineering to produce a football that will stand up to strong forces and perform reliably when it is kicked. Such a ball needs to be perfectly round to reduce air resistance and completely waterproof. It also has to be hard-wearing and tough. To achieve all of these things, a modern football is made of several layers.

The outer cover of the ball is made of moulded shapes that fit together.

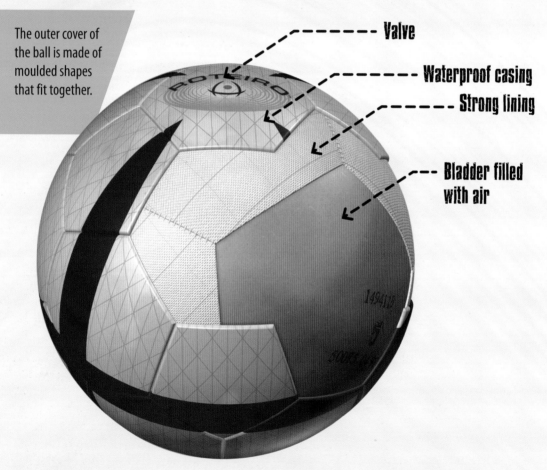

Valve

Waterproof casing

Strong lining

Bladder filled with air

Inside the ball

The core of the ball is a round **bladder** made of **latex**, which is filled with air. Latex is made from rubber or is a **synthetic** material that acts like rubber. The bladder is covered by a strong fabric lining that helps the ball to keep its shape when it is kicked.

The shapes that form the outer cover of a football are produced in a mould to make sure they are identical.

The outer cover

The outer cover is made of strong synthetic material that is cut into shapes that fit together to make a perfectly round ball. In the past, the shapes were sewn together by hand, but modern footballs use a technique called **thermal bonding**. The shapes are fitted into a mould and then heat is used to glue them together. The result is a hard-wearing, waterproof cover.

Testing

The modern design was tested by a robotic football boot to make sure that the ball always performed the same way when it was kicked. Then it was tested by people. They found that the ball was too smooth. As a result, the outer cover was made slightly rough so that it would move more accurately through the air. The next time you play with a football, test how it reacts to the different types of force you use to kick it.

Good ball control

What are the most important skills a footballer needs? To score a goal, it helps to kick the ball fast and accurately, while a goalkeeper uses force to clear the ball far up the field. However, football is a team sport and controlling the ball and passing between players is every bit as important as kicking it with great force.

Passing

Controlling the ball means keeping it close to your feet and passing accurately before you are tackled. First, you have to stop the ball without it rebounding to a player on the other team. Then you use many small forces to keep the ball close to your feet. Before passing, you need to judge how hard to kick the ball and in what direction so that your team mate can run forward on to the ball.

Dribbling and tackling

You may decide to dribble the ball up the field. Then you kick it forwards with a light force and run after it. You may dodge an opposing player by kicking it to one side of them or between their legs. The tackling player tries to get their foot to the ball with enough force to stop the ball and send it in another direction.

Footballers use their hip, knee and ankle joints the most. They need strong muscles in their thighs, glutes, hips and calves.

A player prepares to take a free kick. If he can get the ball past the opposing wall of players, his team may score a goal.

Taking a free kick

Sometimes a free kick is awarded just in front of the goal. Several of the opposing team stand side by side between the ball and the goal to form a "wall". The best kickers can curve the ball by putting a spin on it as they kick, so that the ball goes around the wall and into the goal!

How many different forces?

In most sports and games, several forces are in action at the same time. The result is the sum of all the different forces. In football, gravity, air resistance and wind affect the path of the ball as well as the force and direction of the kick. In tennis, the action and reaction of the racket add another set of forces.

Driving force

The serve is the most powerful force in professional tennis. The action is a bit like that for throwing a ball forwards, but the racket increases the speed. Top players can serve the ball at over 250 kilometres (155 miles) per hour. Ground strokes, where the player hits a forehand or backhand after the ball has bounced, can be powerful too. The player hits a winner when they put the ball beyond the reach of their opponent.

Ball and racket

Tennis balls are filled with air. Hard balls, in which the air is under most pressure, travel furthest and fastest. When a racket hits a fast ball, both the racket strings and the ball are pushed out of shape. Part of the ball is compressed and the strings bend. Both store energy, which returns to the ball to give it extra force for the return.

Fast reactions

Like all sports, tennis involves many skills. The players have to react quickly to guess the path of the ball and be in the right place in time to choose the right stroke. Players use their eyes and brains as well as their muscles and joints to win the game.

direction and speed of ball

Muscles tighten
to produce force
to hit the ball

Serena Williams watches
the ball closely as it speeds
towards her. She is ready to
hit under the ball, to send it
spinning back over the net.

gravity

1 Which of these things is not necessary to run a marathon?
a) good lungs
b) big feet
c) a strong heart
d) strong muscles

2 The pole in a pole vault stores energy when it is bent. This energy:
a) seeps out of the bottom of the pole into the ground
b) makes the pole shake as the pole-vaulter rises into the air
c) returns to the pole-vaulter to give them an extra push
d) stays in the pole

3 Why should a football be perfectly round?
a) to make it more streamlined
b) to make it bounce
c) to make it waterproof
d) to make it bend when you kick it

4 Which joints does a sprinter use most?
a) elbow, neck and knee
b) shoulder, wrist and ankle
c) hip, elbow and neck
d) hip, knee and ankle

5 The force of friction is stronger:
a) on a rough surface
b) on a wet surface
c) going uphill
d) on a smooth surface

6 What forces are acting on a long jumper when he or she is in the air?
a) forward momentum from pushing off the ground and air resistance
b) force of friction from pushing off the ground and gravity
c) gravity and air resistance
d) forward momentum from pushing off the ground, gravity and air resistance

7 Which muscle or muscles are used to straighten your elbow when you throw a ball?
   a) the muscles in your lower arm
   b) the biceps, the muscle at the front of the upper arm
   c) the triceps, the muscle at the back of the upper arm
   d) the muscles in the shoulder

8 In swimming, why does pushing back the water push you in the opposite direction?
   a) because you use the flat of your hand
   b) because when you push the water it pushes back with an equal force in the opposite direction
   c) because water resistance pushes against gravity
   d) because water resistance is stronger than the force pushing the water back

9 Which force helps you to catch and hold on to a ball?
   a) gravity
   b) friction
   c) air resistance
   d) water resistance

10 Streamlining:
   a) reduces gravity
   b) increases water resistance and air resistance
   c) increases friction
   d) reduces water resistance and air resistance

Glossary

aerobic requiring extra oxygen. Aerobic exercise makes you breathe deeper and faster.

air resistance force that slows down the movement of an object through the air

biceps muscle in the upper arm that contracts to bend the arm at the elbow joint

bladder stretchy bag. The core of a football is called a bladder because originally a pig's bladder was used.

compressed squashed or squeezed by a force

contract become shorter

counteract act against a force to reduce its effect

digestive system parts of the body that break down food into the different nutrients that the body needs to survive

effort in a lever, the force used to move the load

energy ability to do work

force force is a push or a pull on an object. A force gives energy to an object.

force meter machine for measuring force. It can also be used to weigh something, since weight is a measure of the force of gravity.

friction force produced when one surface moves over another surface. Friction acts to slow down the movement.

glutes short for *gluteus maximi*, the muscles in the buttocks, the soft parts that cushion your bottom

gravity force of attraction between two objects. On Earth, gravity pulls everything towards the ground. This is because Earth's mass is much greater than everything around it.

hip joint that links the top of the thigh bone to the pelvis, the bone that cradles your lower belly

joint place where two bones meet and fit together. The shape of the joint determines how the bones move.

latex rubbery material that is bendy and slightly stretchy

lever simple machine that magnifies the effect of a force. A lever is a rod or pole that moves around a point to make something move.

load weight that a lever moves

lubricant liquid or grease that makes surfaces smoother and so reduces friction

lungs parts of the body where oxygen from the air moves into the blood and waste carbon dioxide moves from the blood into the air that is breathed out

mass amount of matter, or physical substance, something has. Weight is related to mass because weight measures the force of gravity on the mass of an object.

momentum force of a moving body or object due to its movement. Momentum increases with mass and speed.

muscle soft part of the body that shortens to move a particular bone or part of the body

nutrients parts of food that a living thing needs to grow and be healthy

oxygen one of the gases in the air

pivot point around which a lever turns

reaction force produced in response to another force; reaction is also the way a person responds to an event

rebound bounce in the opposite direction

stamina ability to keep doing something before becoming too tired

streamlined shaped so that air or water moves easily around an object

synthetic material made by people from another material, such as oil

thermal bonding joining two pieces together by coating the edges with glue and heating them so that they melt and become securely attached

triceps muscle at the back of the upper arm that straightens the arm

water resistance force that slows down the movement of an object through water

Find out more

Books

Crushed! Explore Forces and Use Science to Survive (Science Adventures), Louise and Richard Spilsbury (Franklin Watts, 2013)

Cycling (Sports Science), James Bow (Franklin Watts, 2013)

Forces and Motion (Essential Physical Science), Angela Royston (Raintree, 2014)

Websites

www.bbc.co.uk/education/clips/z8jc87h
Go to this section of the BBC's Learning Zone to see how a squash ball is flattened by the force of hitting the wall of the court. Go to the Physical Education section to find lots more information about different sports and sportspeople.

www.fun-facts.org.uk/human_body/muscles.htm
Find out more about muscles and how you use them to move your body.

pbskids.org/sid/funwithfriction.html
Play the game that explores friction on different surfaces with Sid the Science Kid.

www.sciencekids.co.nz/sports.html
The Sports Science for Kids website includes experiments, games, videos and fun facts about various sports and the human body. Click on the rugby video to find out why a rugby scrum is the most dangerous moment in sport.

www.sciencemuseum.org.uk/educators/teaching_resources/activities.aspx
This Science Museum website has lots of science activities, including how to make your own rocket mouse.

Places to visit

Science Museum
Exhibition Road
South Kensington
London SW7 2DD
www.sciencemuseum.org.uk

This is the world's largest science museum of its kind. It has 40 galleries that explore scientific breakthroughs and include hands-on exhibits.

Glasgow Science Centre
50 Pacific Quay
Glasgow G51 1EA
www.glasgowsciencecentre.org

This museum is informative and entertaining. It includes interactive exhibits, workshops, shows and activities. Even the buildings are amazing!

Wimbledon Lawn Tennis Museum
All England Lawn Tennis Club
Church Road
London SW19 5AE
www.wimbledon.com/museum

Wimbledon, the most famous tennis tournament in the world, is played on these courts. The museum includes interactive galleries, film and video of exciting matches and much more.

Football Stadium Tours
Most major football clubs offer tours of their stadium and pitch.

Further research

- You can explore for yourself the important part forces play in any sport. Go to your local library and look online for information about how particular sports are played. See if you can find out how the athletes use and control the various forces.

- Collect as many different types of ball as you can, such as a squash ball, ping-pong ball, golf ball, rugby ball as well as a football and tennis ball. Compare how each one bounces and how they vary in size and weight. See if you can find out why a tennis ball is slightly furry.

- Go to your local sports centre and try one of the sports in this book. Can you use your knowledge of how forces work to improve your technique?

- Go to your local swimming pool and practise making different shapes as you swim. Try keeping your head in line with your back, and your back level. Time yourself to see which shape results in the fastest time.

Index